CHIPPY

THE SEA LION THAT LOST ITS WAY

Written by Christine Haller

Illustrated by Nancy M. Lund

This story is based on a true event.

Copyright © 2006
Oxbow Books
76 Presidio Drive
Novato CA 94949

ISBN 0-9771129-0-X
Library of Congress Control Number: 2005908213

Printed in China by Prolong Press Limited

Dedicated to

Tim, Jameson, and Maddie,
whose love of ocean animals inspired this book

Along the rocky California coast a playful sea lion enjoys floating in pools of white sea foam, swimming in and out of tangles of long green kelp, and diving deep into cold ocean waters in search of tasty squid, herring, and lamprey eel.

He spends hours stretched out on a sandy beach, sometimes nuzzling with a friend or two. His shiny dark brown fur dries to soft cinnamon in the warm sun.

One day, the sea lion swam unexpectedly through the bay, towards the river delta, and into an adventure that captured the hearts of many.

His voyage took him under enormous steel bridges, through busy river channels, and into narrow farmland canals of the Central Valley of California.

When he reached the end of each canal, he quietly climbed up onto the levee, plodded across the dirt road, and slipped into the next canal, unnoticed by passers by.

When the weary traveler finally clambered out of the water at his journey's end and onto a small road next to a field of lettuce, he was nearly 100 miles from his ocean home!

A local farmer driving his pickup truck along a road one morning surprisingly discovered the misplaced sea lion.

"Where did you come from big fellow?" he wondered aloud.
The farmer looked around, saw no water nearby, and rubbed his chin, confused. He called the local emergency dispatch.

"Wait until you see what I just found!" he exclaimed.

California Highway Patrol officers (nicknamed "CHiPs") hurried to the scene and parked their patrol cars alongside the road. After taking in the sight of the wayward coastal visitor, the officers summoned wildlife rescuers for help.

To the astonishment of the officers and the gathering crowd, the hefty sea lion, nicknamed Chippy by his officer friends, lumbered closer and climbed onto the back of the patrol car. Chippy rested on top of the trunk that was warm in the morning sun.

Marine rescue workers arrived with nets, circling around the patrol car to capture the sunning sea lion that bellowed in protest. With the efforts of six men and women, and some tempting with a pail of herring, the 300-pound fellow was corralled into a steel carrier and loaded into the back of a truck for his return journey to the ocean.

Chippy was first examined at The Marine Mammal Center, located on the coast near San Francisco, a place that cares for sick and injured sea lions. Veterinarians worried that he did not eat heartily or play with the other sea lions at the center. They then discovered a gunshot wound in the soft folds of his sturdy neck.

The sea lion received special care and treatment at the Marine Mammal Center. Well wishes and support poured in for him from many people, near and far, and young and old, who had heard the remarkable story of the adventuresome Chippy.

Chippy improved quickly, regained his sizable appetite, and resumed his usual playful ways with the other sea lions that were also recovering at the center. It was time for the sprightly sea lion to return to his ocean home.

One gentle spring day, Chippy was transported to a California beach that had been chosen as the perfect location for his release. He ambled out of the large carrier, lingered to stretch his neck from one side to the other, and then freely made his way down the shore into the vast Pacific Ocean.

Chippy was finally home.

Chippy's travels through the San Francisco Bay and San Joaquin River Delta took place over 3 weeks in February 2004.

After being rehabilitated at The Marine Mammal Center in Sausalito, California, Chippy was released on March 3, 2004. Marine biologists monitored his movements with a satellite transmitter attached to his back to see if he adapted to his return home. The sea lion promptly swam through the Golden Gate, and into San Francisco Bay to join hundreds of barking sea lions sunning on the docks of Pier 39, to the delight of many visitors.

Chippy's journey continued, as days later he was tracked in the San Pablo Bay, and then once again in the Sacramento River delta. Ten days after his release, the transmitter was lost, and the subsequent travels of Chippy are unknown. Marine biologists think that plentiful fish in the river delta lured Chippy back into this now familiar territory.

Acknowledgements

We are grateful to The Marine Mammal Center
and the California Highway Patrol
for their helpful guidance with this book.

About the author

Christine Haller, M.D. is a physician at the University of California, San Francisco. She teaches and conducts clinical research, and is the author of several medical book chapters and scientific articles. She grew up in the San Francisco Bay Area, and now lives with her husband and three children in Novato, California. This is her first children's book.

About the illustrator

Nancy Lund is a theater set and scene artist and graphic designer for the Mayflower Community Chorus in Marin County, California. She resides in Novato, California. This is her first children's book.